WHAT BOOKS PRESS

AN IMPRINT OF

THE GLASS TABLE

COLLECTIVE

LOS ANGELES

# US CLUMSY GODS

ALSO BY ASH GOOD

we are not ready for what we are
sounds in my möbius mind
these things will never happen quite like that again

US CLUMSY GODS

ASH GOOD

WHAT BOOKS PRESS

LOS ANGELES

Copyright © 2022 by ash good. All rights reserved.
Published in the United States by What Books Press,
the imprint of the Glass Table Collective, Los Angeles.

Library of Congress Cataloging-in-Publication Data

Names: good, ash, 1984- author.
Title: us clumsy gods / ash good.
Description: Los Angeles : What Books Press, [2022] | Summary: "The poems
   of us clumsy gods reach for knowing-both attainable and untouchable.
   In ash good's memory/dream of where "we'd be good to each other,"
   clear-edged vessels gravitate into a cosmos of ghosts, danger, trauma,
   pleasure"-- Provided by publisher.
Identifiers: LCCN 2022021013 | ISBN 9781733378918 (trade paperback)
Subjects: LCGFT: Poetry.
Classification: LCC PS3607.O56269 U8 2022 | DDC 811/.6--dc23/eng/20220506
LC record available at https://lccn.loc.gov/2022021013

Cover art: Gronk, *Untitled*, paint on wood door with engraved brass knocker.

What Books Press
363 South Topanga Canyon Boulevard
Topanga, CA 90290

WHATBOOKSPRESS.COM

in loving memory

Bessie Jane Riggs
April 10, 1923–August 13, 2017

William E. Goodwin
August 22, 1934–January 13, 2020

Wesley J. Linder
January 15, 1939–July 10, 2020

Odie Mae Linder
January 7, 1938–April 19, 2021

POEMS

INNER/TERRESTRIALS

sound of *stay* & *grow* comes out of the same mouth	3
my third grade teacher isn't squeamish	6
altar offering to what we cannot know	7
serious child	8
theme park polaroids	9
experiment	10
learning world / reach withdraw	11
what trance parts the sea at its own will?	12
this is what it feels like to love	15
us? beautiful / prepared for our own demise	16
something heroic about curling into a fetal position to hold the multiverse under the bed	18
so many things we must be alone enough for	19
what i apprehend of time travel	20
how small will life be / for how long	22
the realness of body	25
are you ashamed chest still swells when you hear the national anthem?	26
in a multiplying universe we want to touch but	27
everywhere intimate devastations	28
i don't want to be careful	29
i haven't	34
let	36
walking alone	37

**PLANETESIMALS
OR SKIPPING STONES IN ATMOSPHERE**   41

OUTER/GIANTS

but can novelty be our gender?	55
taut center / loose edges	56
let us wake different	57
this is what i will tell them	58
are you in touch with	62
when we master that space between	63
i can already see through skin on the back of my hand	64
i'll do my best to be multilingual	65
look at you baby self	66
you didn't realize this was how shoulders do push-ups	67
we meant for that to happen	68
relieved to be small in a wave that will never relent	69
nothing is stopping us	70
happening everywhere all at the same time	74
if you see us dancing know	75
it takes light years to get around things	76
an entire world depends on you consistently dreaming yourself alive	77
want for beauty that could kill me	80
greedy	84
earth paradise	85
awake	86
we move & stars blur	87

notes	93
sources	98
acknowledgments	100

we share the sky, all of us   —ALBERTO RÍOS

when you look at the stars and the galaxy, you feel that you are not just from any particular piece of land, but from the solar system
—KALPANA CHAWLA

this substanceless substance, this bending and shaping, this warping, this is the way we understand our world   —LOUISE ERDRICH

INNER/TERRESTRIALS

SOUND OF *STAY & GROW* COMES OUT OF THE SAME MOUTH

after Major Jackson

1

let me begin again soft parts out pincers plush & unserrated i am full of easy ways to depart my known body slowly examine misgivings by turning the shells in space Reader i should have warned you we are tender & distracted this time let me be three futures ahead with no grit lost fast-forwarding *i'll be clear* >> i am siphoning invasive desires out of my groundwater spilling them back into lost & found is this yours? did you dream of being a prodigy or savant or mother? i dream & dream textures & aperitifs & flights & revelations not a crumb leaves me hungry to conjure so in some sense not even dreaming in this flickering picture left explainable only to altar— let me begin again by bowing & a confession

2

i wish the evaporated places that shaped me were bottled somewhere corked & labeled so on a quiet weekday morning i could slip unnoticed into my first apartment yellow chandelier earrings << *eventually lost like all earrings* exact in slit of light on record player how purple the gladiolus sometimes i'd go back & slide open auntie's kitchen drawer (two in) for the orange-handled scissors sometimes i'd wait for the smoke heavy in high planks of uncle's cavern to hit my nose or i'd sit in rain humid breezeway back against rough red brick & marvel at how long my legs are now i'm dreaming & i'll be in the present when i wake << *an oddly trustworthy sentence*

3

ask what's real no what's happening no what's true << *synonyms* reasons memory limited by three dimensions isn't reasonable are you too waiting for black hole to spaghettify your body while you force yourself to visit & revisit information before or beyond horizon? Reader i know you can't possibly listen when i utter *stay with me*

                                        we're always in such a rush

MY THIRD GRADE TEACHER ISN'T SQUEAMISH

dissecting a piglet & lets me hold the eyeball & when i am curious about innerworking the teacher cuts it clean open i don't figure out then how that sludge parses light in the back of the classroom incubators hum & i learn which week the beak forms & what those mysterious white globules are attached to yoke this is still a real classroom even though two years ago half this brick school burns while i am wearing overalls pink ruffles hems too long that soak up puddles in a fire drill line even though this is not a drill *this is not a drill*

when i throw eggs off the roof in cardboard & rubber bands engineered by my small hands this is not the first or last time i will need to protect fragile things this is also not the first or last time i will beat a boy who draws dinosaurs better than the ones in my science book whose name i write in a game of M-A-S-H on a notebook page i tell my own future because even a nine year old feels the ache *please jesus something tell me what happens*

ALTAR OFFERING TO WHAT WE CANNOT KNOW

after Lunita Valeria Velásquez

our most tender ghosts are still nameless have yet to reveal origin whole in our ear while we are still at the stove simmering or when it's quieter home alone at rainbow hour dancing between reality prisms we sense apparitions circled in council weathered translucent hands joined & imploring *just let the kiddos play a little longer* our tender ghosts hold us better than we can free them *just be don't worry your head with our heaviness* —only don't you know wise ones?— children hear everything especially when we pretend we are asleep

SERIOUS CHILD

move rocks from pile to pile / all business even if no memory of why / dig hole on tidal sand / fill with salt water / drip out planet's other side / *here is the only rule of make believe* >> choose & trust your collaborators / oh serious child your doubts can topple all kinds of grown-ups / *you don't know these words yet but you'll need them* >> don't entertain my paranoia like a thought you never had / hold me & assure some of this? only nightmare / sort unclear shapes to grok yellow / sound of leaf breathing / what bravery is beholden to / malleable you be unconcerned / with longevity or tying any end down / cartwheel in invisible wake

THEME PARK POLAROIDS

after Ursula K. Le Guin

plump belly / sherbert striped tank / bangs heavy / beside much too-large smurf / unsure why blue smurf as much as why pink shorts / too-rough terry-cloth / urgent on skin decades later / go ahead & say i'm working off memories of *memories* >> twenty-two & envious of gay friends' bodies / easy to dress with such nice calves & drawers full of cargo shorts / nine & learn commitment on coaster's clicking climb / i'm not a person who will stop a ride / but i might close my eyes / i might cry

EXPERIMENT

this is going badly at core idea seed tossed between sorrow-full & joyous child hands reach for hot potato eyes in room brimming & aimed at earth hungry for deus ex machina how long does it take to overwrite fantasies? maybe get to five counting honest-to-god good times << *that's a real data point* we're not going back or forward to claim us we're going in more naked warrior than tactical soldier forgiveness after accountability at nipple of disobedience not aiming to bite only disarm what hurts & hurts & hurts our siblings *you yeah you i love you* we remember what all parents have done & want it to be someone else's racism but find it in our bodies clenched on sidewalk epigenetic fears orphaned lies never pulled at root yours mine ours from inside these processes might feel unnatural & unfair then *holy-shit* we lose all need to behave our way into worth *hypothesis* >> pleasure doesn't need to be earned & sweaty palms also presence let's go to the edge ask why center only thumps hard here why so radical to allow mistakes

LEARNING WORLD / REACH WITHDRAW

fingers stretch / anemone tendrils

ocean / mouth   yawn   return / uncovered

body   jut / rock   puddle   sun / sparkle

cells   breath / die   please

touch / gentle   move

free / fish   wave   crab / shuffle

gray   shadow / slippery   never seen / today

                  i am a tidal pool

bring / galoshes

WHAT TRANCE PARTS THE SEA AT ITS OWN WILL?

> *You said it didn't hurt at all*
> *and let it wash away . . .*
> —Florence + The Machine

weave through crush of bodies / grazing

every part sexy

before fear of strangers / lethal microbiomes

try to pretend > / pleasure & pain: anonymous

it breaks down in a public bathroom

we might tell each other / how pretty we are

with sincerity (we never learned working retail)

in between mirror poses / noticing our own odd vacuums

can we go back to the nineties?

sweets no amount of face glitter or butterfly
clips will hold closed this earth wound now

pass wad under stall / fingertips brush

share lip gloss again / we are invincible

part with no melancholy / briefly

we love each other enough   / where everything is enough

only aren't we extremists?   / over tired over empty over full

over alive

    shame when really all we wanted were good neighbors

you'd play loud music once in awhile

so would i but   / we'd keep a loose count

we'd be good to each other—only   / *current estimate* >>

humans are ingesting a credit-card's-worth

of plastic per week   / micro / macro

all poison   / mutilated or set to be

    baby more than ever we need the music

damn all pries anything from   / unsoothable

child hands   / hiccup sobbing

no you cannot make me—don't make me

turns out we can't   / pull all the splinters

using only our own force   / better help each other bleed

something gives in the pulse &

they did their best but they did not know how to love you

is that the sea ready to part?

THIS IS WHAT IT FEELS LIKE TO LOVE

heaviness slips sun on deck sip turmeric remove socks cannot so easily loosen ribs *it is so many people* when we count to five explain how tight a knot is tied how many worlds fit on a dinner plate? world could be anything but today is five red berry vines warm water neck-deep horizon ripened sunset well-worn path past-life neighborhood small world is legs swinging in shopping cart ruins of chicken coop we're not scared of muddy shoes let it all get too close misplace your rage rabbit fur palms convince body there isn't a sharp thing around breathing night lures us out in sound golden arches pour light through pink bottlebrush blocks from home on los angeles sidewalk spooked noticing feet bare & we are here to track in the whole world

US? BEAUTIFUL / PREPARED FOR OUR OWN DEMISE

Vanport, Ore., Sept. 26, 2020

for awhile we live that revolution
    follow both of them in riot gear
no stopping now i say
    it hits me before it hits me
    oh
how often do i hover just outside

radio crackle / broadcasted warning / proud boys on the move / tension / big fields / stacked cars few exits / locked port-a-johns / dumpster to pee behind

& this is all true

spies / no real names / police / affinity groups tactics / probably guns / visible weapons are a liability / black bodies / so much ballistic armor

maybe even the memory is dangerous—
this dream, that body
convinced of future we may never land in

little we each know to do our part / head-to-toe black bloc but dope sneakers / calls for eye contact & trust gravity / real-time / history / in ribcages / heartbeats

> *i know exactly what this city looks like*
> *i can't shake that i really love you stranger—*
> *have you ever felt more human?*
> *more flawed & unstoppable?*

there is a radiant black woman / live yellow bloom in her bullet proof vest / when i ask you to imagine a flower / the whole thing fits right there in your mind

> *open your eyes*
> *hope you survive*

SOMETHING HEROIC ABOUT CURLING INTO A FETAL POSITION TO HOLD THE MULTIVERSE UNDER THE BED

for Beth

trade known to breathe
    open intercostal portal

        undone rippling
            out of walls

                doors-down neighbors
                  vaguely suspicious

part legs at threshold
    in/out of body

        heavy on another room's floor
        unsure of when/how

            we've time traveled
              to watch ourselves

vital hum in deference
over-swollen

        for fingernails armpit hair
        saliva contained

            in pose of child
              water bearer

to ocean that belongs to us
    our mother

        the being-at-the-market
            we never speak to

SO MUCH WE MUST BE ALONE ENOUGH FOR

if this house is *empty* of lovers if this mind is *empty* of ghosts if this bathtub is *empty* of expectations lungs can be *empty* of guttural sigh *empty* & fit honestly for once in soft skeleton *empty* again pick up identities like golden peaches soft << *likely to bruise* one by one 'til mesh bag far too heavy eggplants argue with limes & we cannot make everyone happy *enough!* drop it all & *empty* out of shopper costume entirely *empty* not a daughter *empty* not a friend *empty* not a lover *empty* not a poet *empty* not a good girl << *suddenly we can breath empty* not an informed citizen *empty* not an example *empty* not alone *finally here* >> space to lift off with roque parking lot birds *empty* open beating *oh.*
sweet craving in sink teeth chin dribbles ripe story *encore/infinity* >> belly so full then rumble *empty*

WHAT I APPREHEND
OF TIME TRAVEL

1

grandfather's twenty-five-year-old cactus blooms
a new flower / african violets endure up to fifty
years / it is so much pressure to care for the plants
of a ghost / can you tell me / who even has only one
phantom / raucous over here / spirits tip pots over
i can live off petrichor / do my best not to prick
myself / at least / not in the same place again

2

i know too much of invisible / love / poison
never catch first rain on my tongue / tell us / *keep
your body pure* & nature helps us fail / all the arms
we have are umbrellas or linked with comrades
we didn't ask for war / we wanted wild / hum / look
through the moan / ask / *is it even mine* / monsoons
roar / small feral sounds look for our mouths

3

we will be sharp with our mothers / even after tarot
admonishes *soften a heart* / yes you / child / gifted
vocabulary / *trauma* / *epigenetic healing* / wail at
your responsibility / be imperfect / reduce harm / start
with bird spikes / bumps that stop sleep / signs that lie
THIS PLACE IS NOT FOR / howl at pleasure / admit
we have all been a pigeon & a tired person

4

you will stir for / before / barbaric past / before
in eden / before / i could touch them / before now
now after / before / not tall enough to reach / auntie's
sink / yellow rose / wallpapered french bathers / now
she is an invisible vessel / among what is hers / looks
over all / i water / drink from / care for / *this is good*
tell me of the apparition / i am / home i protect

HOW SMALL WILL LIFE BE / FOR HOW LONG

plague seems an antique word . . .
—Holaday Mason, "Virus. Virus. I love you."

1

what can be controlled / dish soap label facing forward towel tag unshowing / arrange & rearrange discomfort / vacuum underneath / hollow small corners into temporary grief altars disease whispers in open spring window / sometimes apologizing before shutting off a news cycle / read a headline or light a candle for injustice / does one help more than the other?

2

so i'm thinking again about adaptation / pressure / cosmic storms / veils / but getting carried away *shorthand* >> i've been considering shame & spotless is a task too big storage pile shrinks / body count rises / *have you done enough to deserve existence?* << THE 'F*CK DOES THAT VOICE COME FROM? let our meager empire be sufficient

3

daydream >> us blowing through stop signs in the desert just notice does it require more space or more time space / time / grand canyon implied / space slash time can the slash hold you / in the lapses between me? at some point we come upon the wiki for caesura accusing you poet of being composer of breath / yes

THE REALNESS OF BODY

i wake you / you wake me / cycling fifty-minute-ago alarm / attainable freedom / hair needs brushed / pulled off neck / dry-shampooed / entangled again / clean hair / no texture / i like these snarls but not

yesterday's / ticking time bomb of perfect-length nails one hour too long & talon torn / constant evaluation of thinness / too-loose neck skin / spot may / not be malignant / what do i pretend is real?

only wanted to be / a gentle magician / like you know precisely when i touch your third eye / reply fingerprint dead center palm / is it witchcraft when i see / through you or when i can't?

thrust into 24-hour-a-day performance / flammable & reliant on fire extinguishers / in our war of waking bodies / quivering muscles are rearranging nervous systems / no one taught us to dream or breathe

ARE YOU ASHAMED CHEST STILL SWELLS WHEN YOU HEAR THE NATIONAL ANTHEM?

my radicalized bones daydream i go to the wrong rally undercover really put some time into imagining cute flag tattoo (temporary) on cheek under eye blond hair neat in braids & i already own a patriotic-colored ball cap on accident weird how this whole setup feels like child costume on national holiday & they certainly won't believe i belong & what will i say to people i hate & i don't wanna hate & if i talk at all i won't tell a single lie will i be found out if i say *i am scared for my country it doesn't feel like there is room for us* & what comes of cosplay recon into belly of a white-hooded monster? what goes through my head after skin turning raw to scrub away tiny flag? how do you wash hate out of hair?

IN A MULTIPLYING UNIVERSE
WE WANT TO TOUCH BUT

after Lina Kostenko

nurse in full PPE swings camera to balloons you can do nothing as virus razes body that made body that made your body what's to focus on is *please drink the ensure to get stronger* & gram mumbles you sure are pretty & you want to say *how you brushed my hair taught me hands can land soft on this body* but all confessions are too long when nurse must re-yell each word somewhere a comet flies & on zoom soundless fragments trail zero gravity to ground

EVERYWHERE INTIMATE DEVASTATIONS

after Jenn Lalime

do not reach around this for remote but we are human & at my house we do drink more wine buy every special bottle of whiskey at this point who knows if more will come from japan during fire season i pack what magic i cannot bear to leave & utility silly to abandon into bags resting in bedroom temple of otherwise also irreplaceable but (maybe literally certainly metaphorically) placed on a pyre at this point who knows *a meditation on irreplaceability* >> you cannot be destroyed i cannot be destroyed << *repeat the only prayer we can mouth in this noise* blog advises scrub your sink & keep it clean & you'll feel like a million bucks & i really try & even stay at it for awhile *but this is also a way to love ourselves* >> micro-messes boundless & untidy & it's okay to wanna be held *i mean* >> i believe you when you tell me it is hard

I DON'T WANT TO BE CAREFUL

after Buddy Wakefield & Timmy Straw

1

but if you're not careful you can make an identity of someone else's emergency probably the same person who says *be careful be careful be careful* until it does that thing that words do where the sounds fall apart & lose all meaning & then the emergency (who is not you) will call & say help i've fallen &

2

lost all meaning & this will go on until you build walls & wear earplugs to escape the sirens & tell the emergency of the world to fuck off so you can have a damn minute to be inside your craft in an alley a cheap motel the living room at noon on a tuesday & even then you'll call it privilege to run & run from the multiplying explosions

3

in the rearview mirror if you want to get romantic like that other poet go ahead & say we're all emergencies *i know* this is exhausting & there are techniques for holding more & more (especially in the break between lines) but i am so tired of them or— bored. the real emergency— under it all —emergencies are boring now

4

or can't help but be a subway tunnel a rushing river *again* a morgue truck on backup at a secret location *again* a-town-once-paradise burns to ashes at the end of summer just tell me the truth fires are raging fed up is the way there will always be news & we are full & barely digesting we are not okay
  .

5

we're full full something must hold the emergency
(& god please let it transcend bookends & repetition)
the poem can never be long enough add your line
to the end—   .

I HAVEN'T

1

since the artichoke bloomed / since i was shocked out of my foot bones / since it rained / since sun streamed through the prisms again / since yesterday's nap with the maple / since trumpet guy played in my driveway & a girl's shoulder oozed from less-lethal weapons & i gave away every cold la croix in the fridge to protester cheers *viva la revolucion* / not since the ash starting falling again since the wind growled over the dinnerplate dahlia / since i accidentally sprayed myself full-tilt with the hose / i haven't since the fire caught / not since that first hug in months

2

when it's been this long & a dam breaks / do you too wonder *is this pain or pleasure?* / if i were trying to make a friend feel better i would say *you are good despite this gnawing pressure to be supernatural* / here have a recipe to laugh cry feel write / get semi-alone & settle in the dark / exalted & also kneeling to yourself usually it's enough to say one basic truth out loud / i am a person sitting on a floor / in a body i work so hard to know / in a space i have curated to call home

LET

yourself turn belly down held by gravity atop another body LET other soften weight to tether you LET it be dark LET yourself be uneasy LET go of beast you imagine prowls closer LET your eyes rest LET toes curl LET sigh out LET trout of expectation thrash out of river LET funeral tears embrace laughter LET guilt be zeroed LET jetsam leak meaning LET yourself destroy meaning LET yourself destroy yourself if you must LET dark be where you repair LET snow interrupt cherry blossoms LET yourself be

WALKING ALONE

Salmon River at Three Rocks

greet this place aloud *hello* tender *hello* is doorway to prayer is doorway to song move through winged trill waterfall trickle gravel crunch suddenly startle *you might be seen* someone might come upon you strange person hand recklessly on breastbone as luxury fits in the world emerge from domestic rainforest to ocean-mouthed riverbed palm sand's tidal indents until shape of coast one more line on your body aren't vapors whirling above your own mind all around patterned & dancing right there your anemone heart clenching when provoked even by gentle curious touch here shell you outgrew & there you're honed beach-log smooth by turmoil throw yourself on the fire miracle you barely smolder arrive to where you chuckle silly you thinking yourself stranger that earnest *hello*

PLANETESIMALS OR SKIPPING STONES IN ATMOSPHERE

a cento

                                    1
                         apart from their
                   rapid movement they appeared
                         indistinguishable
                            from stars[1]

                                                    2[2]
                                                perpetual
                                        wanderers[3] / come
                            from the forest[4] / the tiny void inside
                                a pod[5] / holds the earth that's
                                    holding[6] / a once-god
                                    hiding[7] / nowhere: far away[8]
                            like a third hand they rearrange[9]
                            the familiar shape[10] / start recognizing
                                    their heart their skin[11]

---

[1] "Asteroid belt" read on *Wikipedia* on June 8, 2021.
[2] Lines spoken at Bloom Open Mic on November 22, 2020.
[3] "Jack walked along the spiral path…" read by the author Paul Deandra.
[4] "I come from the forest" by Andra Schwarz, read by the translator Caroline Wilcox Reul.
[5] "In Some Impossible Mirror" read by the author Lauren Paredes (original line "the tiny void inside a pot").
[6] "She Majestic Tree" read by the author Angela Braxton-Johnson.
[7] "The Tree" by Anis Mojgani, read by Gabby Hancher.
[8] "I can't find them" by Andra Schwarz, read by the translator Caroline Wilcox Reul.
[9] "I forget my voice" by Andra Schwarz, read by the translator Caroline Wilcox Reul.
[10] "The Tree" by Anis Mojgani, read by Gabby Hancher.
[11] "The Secret to Surviving Sinkholes" read by the author Bryan Franco (original line "starts recognizing their heart their skin").

3[12]

this is also based on

a true story[13] / there's wilding

& wilding[14] / i am

the creator[15] / will you be soft

against me?[16]

4[17]

we are the same age[18]

as the future[19] / the cause of all these

mass graves[20] / sings into our twisted guts[21] / i cannot

help but[22] / bless it too[23] / the heroism

is yours[24]

---

[12] Lines written & spoken at Set Your Stories Free writing practice on June 9, 2020.
[13] ahuva s. zaslavsky.
[14] Beth Melnick.
[15] ahuva s. zaslavsky.
[16] ash good.
[17] Lines written & spoken at Set Your Stories Free writing practice on August 24, 2021.
[18] Beth Melnick (original line "I was the same age").
[19] Beth Melnick (original line "what will the future taste like?").
[20] Andra Vltavín.
[21] Beth Melnick (original line "sing into his twisted gut").
[22] ash good.
[23] Andra Vltavín.
[24] Andra Vltavín (original line "the heroism is hers").

5[25]

don't

stop but do rest[26] / not

a thing made sense

& anything could happen next[27] / every memory

breaks off somewhere[28]

6[29]

soaking in vitamin d from

a dashboard[30] / a trunk of tiring

habits[31] / on a tethered raft[32] / past

the galaxies that have

names[33] / what is left

of me?[34]

---

[25] Lines spoken at Bloom Open Mic on April 25, 2021.
[26] "Staring at this exponential graph...." read by the author Andra Vltavín.
[27] "Poem to Be Published Line by Line Along the State Highway System in the Manner of Burma-Shave Advertising" read by the author Dan Wiencek.
[28] "Archeology: A Beginner's Guide" read by the author Dan Wiencek.
[29] Lines written & spoken at Set Your Stories Free writing practice on February 9, 2021.
[30] Andra Vltavín.
[31] Betsy Fogelman Tighe.
[32] Rhonda Nichols.
[33] Andra Vltavín.
[34] Andra Vltavín.

7[35]

i can drift

pretty far away[36] / the challenge

is to walk through the doorway

& this involves crossing the threshold[37] / some of us said

yes some of us said no some of us said

sometimes[38] / these are all

possibilities[39]

8[40]

how can a body stand

this[41] / millenia of impulses[42] / build this

sanctuary from memory[43] / forget yourself regularly[44]

soon you must go[45]

[35] Lines spoken at Open Circle community satsang on March 20, 2021.
[36] Emily Dempsey.
[37] "5 of Cups" in *Dalí. Tarot*, read by ash good.
[38] Andra Vltavín.
[39] "5 of Cups" in *Dalí. Tarot*, read by ash good.
[40] Lines written & spoken at Set Your Stories Free writing practice on September 22, 2020.
[41] "The Thing Is" by Ellen Bass, read by Beth Melnick.
[42] Beth Melnick.
[43] ash good.
[44] Andra Vltavín (original line "forget you regularly").
[45] Rhonda Nichols (original line "soon I must go").

9 [46]

you know what to do[47] / if

you have a

choice[48]

10 [49]

poke your finger

into[50] / deaths little

& large[51] / go down on your butt & wrists[52]

know what you know[53] / make an embarrassing

confession[54] / i do think

that's how to start[55]

---

[46] Lines spoken at Bloom Open Mic on February 28, 2021.
[47] "Or Is It Music?" read by the author Paul Deandra.
[48] "If You Have a Choice" read by the author Emily Moon.
[49] Lines written & spoken at Set Your Stories Free writing practice on June 1, 2021.
[50] Rhonda Nichols.
[51] Beth Melnick.
[52] Rhonda Nichols (original line "go down on my butt and wrists").
[53] Beth Melnick.
[54] Beth Melnick (original line "this is an embarrassing confession").
[55] Emily Dempsey.

11[56]

this

is an antidote[57]

laugh &

it moves the whole room[58] / then make a

beeline[59]/ in the hollow of your

ribcage[60] / a museum

of love[61] / god you are

beautiful[62] / on this minnow of

an earth[63]

---

[56] Lines spoken at Bloom Open Mic on January 24, 2021.
[57] "If You're Still Standing" read by the author Peg Edera.
[58] "Tomorrow Is a Place" by Sanna Wani, read by Andra Vltavín (original line "she laughs and it moves the whole room").
[59] "The Day Will Come" read by the author Peg Edera.
[60] "The Gallery" read by the author Steven Hancher.
[61] "This World is a Museum of Love" read by the author Peg Edera.
[62] "Party House" read by the author Paul Deandra (original line "god they were beautiful").
[63] "In This Place: An American Lyric" by Amanda Gorman, read by Rebecca Dempsey.

12 [64]

hungry mouth

wide open[65] / all the monsters we ever

ran from[66] / slowly let in spring[67] / go ahead & you try[68]

the ocher fields will expand[69] / your brain

a landscape[70] / your crying's music

to their ears[71] / all things are simple

& alive & you may

touch[72]

---

[64] Lines spoken at Bloom Open Mic on December 27, 2020.
[65] "Summer Gestures" read by the author ahuva s. zaslavsky (original line "hungry mouth was wide open")
[66] "Hindsight is sometimes 20/20 or…" read by the author Emily Moon.
[67] "After the Winter" read by the author Angela Braxton-Johnson (original line "slowly letting in spring").
[68] "The Great Regression" read by the author ahuva s. zaslavsky.
[69] "Summer Gestures" read by the author ahuva s. zaslavsky.
[70] "Your Brain a Landscape" read by the author Andra Vltavín.
[71] "Motion" by Wisława Szymborska, read by ahuva s. zaslavsky.
[72] "And will they ever come…" by Lea Goldberg, translated by Rachel Tzvia Back & read by ahuva s. zaslavsky.

13[73]

this is not me telling you

this is rare

science[74] / little vessels of magic[75] / are pregnant with

want & that is

good[76]

14

don't let

the fancy name fool you—

a *celestial* body is anything floating around

in space[77]

---

[73] Lines written & spoken at Set Your Stories Free writing practice on April 28, 2020.
[74] ahuva s. zaslavsky.
[75] Alicia Hazen.
[76] Emily Dempsey.
[77] "6 out-of-this-world celestial bodies you need to know" read on *CBC Kids* on June 9, 2021.

15[78]

dandelion seeds[79] / don't mind

being used as weapon[80] / take shape &

form & land into[81] / all the doors wide open

just for me[82] / by me i mean

you[83]

16[84]

we are not entirely

without resources[85] / call it

your desert heart[86] / body ripe

for the earth[87] / from primordial ooze[88]

we always land with what we bring[89] / the almost

synced sound of our shared watching[90]

your plumage over my rust[91] / makes a liar out of

the night sky[92]

---

[78] Lines written & spoken at Set Your Stories Free writing practice on April 28, 2020.
[79] Beth Melnick.
[80] Andra Vltavín.
[81] Alicia Hazen.
[82] ahuva s. zaslavsky.
[83] Andra Vltavín.
[84] Lines spoken at Bloom Open Mic on October 25, 2020.
[85] "Regarding Eileen Myles" read by the author Paul Deandra.
[86] "Fireside" read by the author Andra Vltavín.
[87] "When You Are a Body" read by the author Gabby Hancher.
[88] "All I want is to be here, just here…" read by the author Steven Hancher.
[89] "Vortex of Forgotten Things" read by the author Emily Moon.
[90] "Like an Autotune of Authentic Love" by Carmen Giménez Smith, read by Andra Vltavín.
[91] "How is it that you keep coming back around…" read by the author Steven Hancher.
[92] "Heaven Lies" read by the author Paul Deandra.

17 [93]

why make stuff up

when someone else says it[94]

our neck of the cosmos[95] / so bright

& yet so small[96]

18 [97]

i wonder

if you were here

during the time i lived here[98] / we are made

of animal bones[99] / everything inside & outside

disputes this message[100] / to hold the change[101] / in the light

of the anthropocene[102] / i can pretend

i'm not human[103] / my brain has never been so extinct[104]

am i doing this right?[105]

---

[93] Lines spoken at Bloom Open Mic on October 25, 2020.
[94] "Regarding Eileen Myles" read by the author Paul Deandra.
[95] "How is it that you keep coming back around…" read by the author Steven Hancher.
[96] "All I want is to be here, just here…" read by the author Steven Hancher.
[97] Lines spoken at Bloom Open Mic on June 27, 2021.
[98] "Note to Laura Hershey After Reading 'If Faith'" read by the author Emily Moon.
[99] "we are not prey" read by the author Gabby Hancher.
[100] "If Faith" by Laura Hershey, read by Emily Moon.
[101] "The Undertaking" by Toi Derricotte, read by Ash Good.
[102] Colette Chien.
[103] "after Jenny Xie, zuihitsu—" read by the author Colette Chien.
[104] "On Top of the Earth Resting in Uncertainty" read by the author Colette Chien.
[105] "after Jenny Xie, zuihitsu—" read by the author Colette Chien.

19 [106]

the record skips[107]

we were born in opposition[108] / here

let me show you this narrative in

my body[109] / stars & mistakes[110] / every good

skipping stone plumbs the depths

eventually[111]

---

[106] Lines written & spoken at Set Yuur Stories Free writing practice on October 5, 2021.
[107] Beth Melnick.
[108] Beth Melnick.
[109] Andra Vltavín.
[110] Beth Melnick.
[111] Beth Melnick.

OUTER/GIANTS

BUT CAN NOVELTY BE OUR GENDER?

for Andra

i text mid-night   you reply   !!!!!!!!!! *ha if it can be that's what*
i am   in daylight our soft anatomy is unambiguous   at collins beach
for respite from revolution   questioning   *when is right to rest? what*
is right to do?   pulled between neck-high submersions in fast-moving river
& crawling back goosebumps to sun   my body bare & warming   your skin
dancing in ink that won't wash   charcoal fingerpainted from found firelog
leaf-filtered light exactly how i like

                        imperfection abounds but here you are
a renewed sliver of sublime creature to soak in   novel   ballcap half-hiding
gaze   child chases father   splashes water   bottoms less bronze than
tangled limbs   my ankle still bruised from less-lethal ammunition   i can't forget
outside forces intend to separate   skin from element   skin from
skin   sand   water   curious fly   body   creation   origin
perfection   what isn't

                    we can't ignore when wind picks up or what lies
ahead   i'm collarbone deep in the unknown again   you offer myths
our past selves wrote to tend our future   i don't know where i came from
but i do know   during this very long week   naked by the columbia
is the closest i'm getting back to it   when we first get here you say
we've come so far   *this might as well be another realm*
& it is

TAUT CENTER / LOOSE EDGES

    pulled / in

                                           severed / stem

             gerbera sips

      caress / petal

                smooth creased
               breathing dissolving
                  young ancient

                                      all i also am

savor a guiltless tryst

                             re: fidelity >>

           our cosmos

                       never asked

LET US WAKE DIFFERENT

not / lover / mother / other / promise / keeper / sweeping / maple's / mess / ego / medicine / burrow / together / dream-deep / in / marrow / unknown / what / weathers / freeze / where / green / copters / seed / who / we'll / be / roots / lifting / foundation / potential / over-winters / among / frosted / fiddleheads / amanitas / warm / trunks / untricked / crave / more / birdsong / before / rousing / daffodils / sun / hydrangeas / chant / we / still / know / life / tulips / rise / defiant / rest / clatters / on / late / morning / orbit / eyelash / rousing / freckle / stirring / closed-eye / murmurs / our / small / asks

THIS IS WHAT I WILL TELL THEM

1

according to my astrological ~~heart~~ *i mean chart* the wounded healer is half human half beast & i have a talent for blurry binaries in the past i've tried to make this not my story said *it won't be easy this way* but you try to quell the sound of hoofs midair you try to patch the holes i can't see wind or what makes a mess or sorts piles at its own whim

2

20% of mental health depends on vacuuming or sweeping sometimes you think i am offering a metaphor & i am not you cut me & i loose ~~a poem~~ *i mean blood* in blooms as i blot & blot what you've opened & i fold & find a clean spot & blot i am a mess & as hard as i try not to make a thing of a mess there in pile of napkins a rorschach

3

cells oxidizing & ~~haunted by~~ *i mean blessed with* meaning i keep a strobilus next to the books to remind much of this smarter than us follow it back to its origin but don't stop some other thing grew the source material or concocted the ingredients in a laboratory or other if you point & say fractal i'll say *have you ever ate acid sat on a curb under a streetlight*

4

& held a pinecone? fuck man the whole tree is in there the. whole. tree. & you say yeah & when pinecones get warm they open— didn't know it was based on heat but makes sense when i get warm i open small tap enrages or i'll accuse you of being sticky *don't touch* like we all don't have sap on our ~~heart~~ *i mean hands* & a damn forest itching inside

ARE YOU IN TOUCH WITH

gay man inside you craving to fall in love in a refined way & hot popular queen who wants to be pursued & mousy one behind glasses lusting to trace labyrinth halls of mind overlap & the witch in you itching to lay hands & digest all knowing of past & potential & sad sensitive girl waiting with umbrella doing her best to keep rain & leaves & love from pulverizing again & there is likely a pragmatic lesbian in there who has done newness too many times can't help but raise an eyebrow at your date who says *home might be a person* she might reach through your arms shake some shoulders & shout *YES—any hope of home has only been your own heart beat even in that first instant two bodies deep* are you in touch with your omniscient voice-over fingers-crossed someone is crushing on you narrator witnessing this ruckus?

WHEN WE MASTER THAT SPACE BETWEEN

after Andra Vltavín

i like to live in the grayzone

i like it i will say

by that name

you will say

experience of you

rather holy unsensible

i have not known

through

whims

when you ask if

i cannot remember it

labels are trouble for me

that sounds accurate to my

androgyny not this not that

you haven't known me long

anything long only i've been

voids enough to entertain decorating

when to lock a door or let a ghost in

I CAN ALREADY SEE THROUGH SKIN ON THE BACK OF MY HAND

veins resemble auntie's ninety-six exquisite now very new seven party daddy misses comes back palm open baby earlobe sparkles make up for it *i* want to keep this cycle of dropping leaves long naps coming back to life turning nine feather crown sure who looks knows *i* come from stars full of history & premonition drawn from the same well is surface tension the threshold of present can *i* throw pennies into past to revise *i* keep seeing kaleidoscope faces same birthday decorations one degree different how many times do *i* turn eleven *i* am in my next body entirely mama gives her summer baby the world again artichoke bloom big as a head royal purple prickly as *i* can be baskets of farm-fresh blackberries raspberries arms full *i* pretend too much *i* am not a time traveler do you wonder how often we find each other freshly-showered chipped nail polish cross-legged on the couch *i* live every age now casual in this body

I'LL DO MY BEST TO BE MULTILINGUAL

laugh cry emoji = dead skull = try to keep up when language is closest we got to unsolidified future young person spill what's tired & i'll listen (even when you say *my favorite band is weezer . . .*

. . . they were very popular in 2008 but definitely making a comeback) << a long pause doesn't always mean you should explain & weezer's first multi platinum album dropped in 1994 but anyway— i will listen & resist pulling you toward this cave of what i can't say yearning to divulge landscapes you won't be able to hear i know because i've been unable to hear so let's wander as we poke what's squishy or not in shared vocabulary it's always uncomfortable on cusp of not being baby we'll eventually learn to live without all the attention i am listening tell me what you see let's cospeak slang of unexpected adaptation bored of all clinging

LOOK AT YOU BABY SELF

in the mirror / bathroom by gym / closest to darkroom closest to the theater / quickest from freshman locker still ugly brown tile / new sink / fresh paint same drab door swings light / backpack heavy / shoulder tuck slump into resistance / before life pushes open / too-big cracks in privacy panels / always straight to largest not wanting closed in / caged regardless / endless hallway / baby angst / dragging feet / no way to know ourself yet / hard way our mind hits mirror every damn exit / oh baby self let's just take a / sweet jesus / hide in a stall minute here / today / look in an old mirror / i see you

YOU DIDN'T REALIZE THIS WAS HOW SHOULDERS DO PUSH-UPS

hot smell & sweat & make a date with yourself to pull weeds find respite in the overgrown hedge & try a taller bike seat & less likely to target fixate & sweet mouse live trap & how many traps tricked you & sun honey sticky sand clings take your body to the river & white crane steals your breath & you want to fly low past your own reflection just once & you can be patient moving at different speeds & just another minute to be in this painting & sigh at soft touch & no guaranteed entry ticket & life drawing finally makes some sense & always time for a sip if you're thirsty & ice water will help your puffy eyes & lock your gaze where you need to land & stick out a hand to slow down & pull in your arms when you want to spin faster

WE MEANT FOR THAT TO HAPPEN

every so often / no pale whorl blurred upper corner no over-opened eyes in the selfie / no selfie / somehow we breathe into clay & *surprise* >> soaring thing escapes untouched / our palms nearly dissolved now / pray tell / how the vanishing occurs? we have photo evidence of our prior existence / wet / sandy / looking at our hands *about the images* >> all that can be said is we strangely didn't know our own power in that moment we disappearing creatures want ocean to recall holding us ocean doesn't care / nothing deserves to exist << *this is grace* if the ancient prayer is disinterest might as well rest & insist ocean's gotta notice / how it falls / when one of us / clumsy gods / drags ourselves out

RELIEVED TO BE SMALL IN A WAVE THAT WILL NEVER RELENT

I touch my own skin, and it tells me that
before there was any harm, there was miracle.
—adrienne maree brown

only one pair of orange eyes in under thicket of rage & hard to get breath into belly even harder to breathe through boot soles to get breath into earth under pavement under temples to far-off power & history swamped at our ankles now eye-level no way to see or understand from inside voice shouts *take a deep breath & remember you can trick your body into thinking it's breathing—* let little sips of air out *slowly remember when the gas comes walk don't run remember* pulsing *remember* why this necessary *remember* why it needs your whole body adjust your privilege gas mask fogging nettle buzzes *stay together stay tight we do this every night* one doesn't want to be singled out no saviors & even if one appears they'll be thwarted by paranoia ulcers or our own government trust we will not look away we are made of uncountable white-hot sins & take grievance prone skin eyes flood

NOTHING IS STOPPING US

1

can we agree a good poem slays all that came before only to strengthen some institution of meaning & there's always someone standing too long in front of the salad greens? spiritual practice is keep our hands on our own damn cart but what i really want to write about is impatience as we hover midair & contorted arms outstretched for earth & spines have never bent like this & no wonder our necks are sore

2

begging *time do your job contain give us something dependable*
afterall sixty seconds is a minute & sixty minutes is an hour
& ten thousand hours makes an expert & how do we trust
in a crisis of zero egress sit still while cities decimated
pin-prick blackholes multiply to gulp another person's sun
let's just swallow our own suns for safe keeping it's been
so long since we flew anywhere that wasn't astral remind us

3

we climbed down from trees gradually & if you think you're invisible someone is thinking of you right now i guess when we die we can care more about being forgotten or how we're remembered or maybe don't waste time on either if we careen wildly off these ropes do we slip into percolating body or is it dark how thick is skin between dimensions either way i imagine we hear thrum of small wet frogs

4

while we're stuck let's write letters that speak of the world to what already squeezed out through the door *dear you i cut lilacs from mama's yard & wasn't going to stop but car pulled itself right & my palms are itchy on cut grass clearing your headstone* mount saint helens sentinel gunpowder light explodes through doug firs *& nothing is stopping us we can feel our hearts here it hurts but we feel our hearts*

HAPPENING EVERYWHERE ALL AT THE SAME TIME

every long-necked bird lifting off blue green earth *every* cotton boll plucked *every* tent stake pounded in by rock *every* uncertainty *every* chin-dribbling bite of watermelon *every* accidental friend bender *every* skipped class *every* caught breath *every* fast corner in a convertible *every* patient smile *every* wallet stolen by a monkey *every* missing knee-high sock *every* scratched itch *every* last shower beer *every* snagged hangnail *every* bridesmaid's toast *every* blistered heel *every* 4 am engine rev heard a mile in all directions *every* sunday rest *every* sex talk *every* queer baby coming out *every* strand of hair tucked behind ear *every* maybe *every* wander off into distraction *every* best done *every* ancestor watches

IF YOU SEE US DANCING KNOW

after Lunita Valeria Velásquez

we think too hard & too much about how frightening to wear such naked joy when did you learn body smile seen may be unfairly seized *this toy is not yours!* we are done fighting over scraps of happiness stop saying *i don't dance* we want to dance with you to brazilian beats in the kitchen while thighs sizzle haze of cedar incense no light but candles lies all drip off now *if you see us dancing know* >> we want the same thing to move us & we're trying to find a fish in our spine that's been here longer than we have how can we flow through this room body like water is all we know what it is to move up current it never was a hunt do you recall the day you learned the word *repeat* you have always known the mission *again* >> wade into swollen stream of ready-to-birth vertebrates *muscle memory* >> migration patterns fissure bone

IT TAKES LIGHT YEARS TO GET AROUND THINGS

for Sierra

maybe you materialize grown on an island with your best friend out for hours without parents to ask *where have you been?* call you to dinner before you are ready stroke sun-kissed cheeks maybe you notice a tween posse of vacation friends all flamingo knees socks slopped down different lengths tumble past in holy childhood mission pretend skystory portals dancing lobster girl god head moving through cloud doors (maybe you only soften decades later to your mother's best attempts) unsure now if watched or watcher maybe you let yourself erupt joy creature pink lips baby teeth gaps giggles until small voice hesitates to squeak *are we normal?* snort-laugh & promise *no!* to wind as it blows through your ribs into ear of curled inner kid *thank heavens we're weird & someday maybe we forgive*

AN ENTIRE WORLD DEPENDS ON YOU CONSISTENTLY DREAMING YOURSELF ALIVE

1

soft neck skin at once a promise of mercy & power satiated bear deep in forest belly full of blueberries so will not devour only there will come a time when you want to be devoured but these are millisecond universes of thought & desire or talking yourself out of doing what your body wants at least twice today

2

if an admission of love is filled with fear you might consume them it's okay to rage *i am not a bear or female praying mantis for that matter* in some tongues everything is hesitant at back of throat elsewhere eager you cannot count the languages necessary be weary of any hint you are not the main character or worse—

3

they might insist *you are intimidating* especially just sitting in your own power a little sweaty early winter late morning on top of hips on a wednesday you can only know yourself from the inside out explain the view of venus to venus & it can't help but feel foreign how can a planet know the bramble of its own skin?

WANT FOR BEAUTY
THAT COULD KILL ME

1

when i paint my face considering light/shadow turns miniscule not nostril but 37 rhombuses peach not quite peach burnt sienna navy magenta grey-green fuzzy edges i finger moss craving it couture gown hugging small of back— mine or at least sublime body hungry for my touch

2

i'm sorry what were you were saying? i was in the sky smelling mysterious lavender absorbing exotic intimacy of ladybug motoring over my knee scratching my scalp until it turns percussion countless small wars erupt from fingertips taunt me again mars it won't take much

3

we'll be at battle i am humbled not by creator but to be creator & damn here's the longest bow you'll give/receive forehead anchored at your own feet stumble into at least three extra dimensions & birth not bodies but beauty-creation itself find hyphens anti-humility fire-child light-rich

4

everyday-god in this equity sweat project keep asking for what you need *whoa slow* let things ripen but also apologize quickly is beauty such vile expectation from all of it sprung into being for no purpose later you'll say *we used every bit of the light* & it isn't a lie we're still here licking our fingers

GREEDY

long to live / forever / stunned / silent / plump body iridescent fly / red tulip / hour maybe week / month nothing but delicate / pattern / transparent / wing / endless superpower / hunger / enhance / until eye contact but with ALL five fly eyes / did you know fly has five eyes? imagine simultaneous vision / 1 fly / 2 hair wind-strung 3 unquarantined love / 4 wy'east distant / 5 child inside reaching hand to fly / oh to be small / curious / smaller make me invisible / unless someone looks closer / sometimes already unseen until / you look closer / all of it beautiful cannot want / another hour / odd / crave ALL i have

EARTH PARADISE

but it was handy pouches of manzanilla olives stuffed in backpacks to fend off blood sugar crashes & shared eyeglass rag when eager greasy prints smudged every view & loud cackles we forgot to be self-conscious of & racquetball rolled under tight tendon anti-itch cream nearby when needed & luxury of dented garage fridge for drinks & leftovers & all that holds elated gasp stomaching cliff it was surprise of allium bursting purple how we trusted we understood or were understood & as we approached the heart of the artichoke it was the fresh cool rapture in our mouths

AWAKE

after Julia Bray

no time / for sheep / name beings / who heal across futures / pasts / great distance / endless list certain / to defeat insomnia / do not count ones who believe / they are healers << *short list awake in the dark* / don't let it be some secret / we rely on cosmic back-up / what appears on time from some other place / I BELIEVE IN YOU << *do we need any other belief at all?* lapping ocean / YOU & YOU & YOU / *new dream* >> us / unshakable / sure / don't you hear the same song / we never mistake ourselves for imposters again

WE MOVE & STARS BLUR

1

pendulum swings overshoots zenith mirage behind mirage ahead so tracks here present mirage & i want you to know you live a good life in this place of refrigerators & road noise & drone & drone bored of manicure of surroundings hungover on uncertainty cells away from sloughing off another year *come with me let's leave*

2

living to pilgrim again all roots hungry & find a city where we know we are wanted *baby when we get there it'll be so different we won't recognize it* bed unmade ripples delicious it rains & i will make the breakfast each one of you asks for three different plates not one compromise we've practiced being hurt for a long time

3

it's that voice again that says call your trauma wound
gaze falls to time-traveling floor grief off-course around
belly bends again hard at sternum heart fern tightly
curled don't obsess over the spiral it's tricky when we
rub only by existing & some plants exert stress hormones
if touched & we use all we got to sense where we stop

4

& crow call begins the sound of healing is sometimes unbelievable far-off voice interrupts *wait isn't it beautiful* we can do nothing but what is required for life *receive* processions of grief visitors with clear intentions *release* when fire is panther then water is octopus air is crane earth is katydid & we repeat ourselves

5

we repeat ourselves about time to call satiation exhaustion don't stop long to obsess we change anyway where we finally rest clean windows & sun stuns we'll remember the song that plays lay with universes on the backs of eyes & if i could finally introduce myself right i would say *for just one minute can we be in love?*

~

NOTES

Page 3—"sound of *stay* & *grow* comes out of the same mouth" was first drafted immediately after reading Major Jackson's "Let Me Begin Again." The lines "Let me begin again" and "Reader, I should have" are Jackson's.

Page 6—"my third grade teacher isn't squeamish" is shared with warmth for my Mrs. Eddy, my science-loving teacher at McBride Elementary.

M-A-S-H (Mansion, Apartment, Shack or House) is a childhood paper-and-pencil fortune telling game played to cheekily predict the outcomes of one's life: where you will live, who your spouse will be, what kind of car you will drive, how many kids you will have, etc.

Page 7—"altar offering to what we cannot know" was written in ceremony on 2019's vernal equinox after a live reading by Lunita Valeria Velásquez of her poem "the skeletons have been coming out." The line "our most tender ghosts" is Velásquez's.

Page 9—"theme park polaroids" taps my own childhood memories after reading "Leaves" by Ursula K. Le Guin which presents the churning question: "What does it mean to say I am that child in the photograph…?"

Page 11—"learning world / reach withdraw" was written after a trip with my three young nieces to the tidal pools surrounding Haystack Rock in Cannon Beach, Oregon—traditional and ancestral lands of the Clatsop and Chinook tribes. This popular seastack on the Oregon coastline is the third-tallest such intertidal structure in the world.

Page 16—"us? beautiful / prepared for our own demise" includes lines drawn from workshop collaboration with Andra Vltavín, Emily Dempsey and Rhonda Nichols including: "and this is all true," "for a while we live that revolution," "follow both of them in riot gear," "no stopping now i say" and "it hits me before it hits me." The lines "when i ask you to imagine / a flower / the whole thing fits right there in your mind" were inspired by the thought labor of Elaine Scarry in *Dreaming By the Book*.

This poem recounts one of the high-tension points of 2020 protests and counter-protests that erupted throughout Portland, Oregon—traditional and ancestral lands of the Multnomah, Clackamas, Chinook, Kathlamet, Tualatin Kalapuya, Molalla and many other tribes and bands of the Columbia and Willamette regions. On September 26, dueling rallies were mounted in the outskirts of the city as The Proud Boys—designated a hate group by the Southern Poverty Law Center—claimed thousands of its members would gather at Delta Park. In response, leftist and Black Lives Matter supporters organized a counterdemonstration in historic Vanport—now the site of Portland International Speedway and adjacent to Delta Park.

Oregon Public Broadcasting would later report, "A much larger crowd of counterdemonstrators to the Proud Boys rally gathered at the Vanport site in North Portland to discuss racial justice Saturday. Speakers talked about the history of Vanport, a town that once housed a large part of Oregon's Black residents but was wiped out in a catastrophic 1948 flood. Racist policies of the time had concentrated many African Americans in Vanport as they worked on shipbuilding efforts during World War II. After the disaster, discriminatory housing policies made it difficult for many of the people who lived in the community to resettle."

Police presence was at an all-time high near the two rallies and across the city at large as a 100-plus car protest crawled the streets and an additional BLM rally overflowed Peninsula Park. While (thankfully) that particular Saturday never resulted in the mass violence city leaders and citizens feared, activists were primed for danger. Especially on-site during the speeches at historic Vanport, risk hummed electric in the air.

Page 20—"what i apprehend of time travel" was written for my paternal great-aunt Bessie Jane Riggs (April 10, 1923–August 13, 2017).

Page 27—"in a multiplying universe we want to touch but" was written after "Chernobyl Poems" by Lina Kostenko (translated by Uilleam Blacker). The line "a comet flies" is Kostenko's. It was reading Blacker's translation of Kostenko's poem that opened some doorway to write about the tragic—at that moment in time oddly universal—experience of communicating via video call with my maternal grandmother, Odie Mae Linder (January 7, 1938–April 19, 2021), while she was hospitalized with Covid-19.

Page 28—"everywhere intimate devastations" came after reading the lines "In my house there were always enough / clean towels, hot food, wine to drink" from Jenn Lalime's poem "Salvation."

Page 29—"i don't want to be careful" was written after reading Timmy Straw's poem "Copernicus," which offers the line "someone else's emergency makes the poem hold."

"That other poet" referred to in my text is Buddy Wakefield, author of the widely-known spoken word performance "We Were Emergencies."

Page 34—"i haven't" was the first poem I was able to write after a span of months where I experienced several particularly violent interactions while protesting (both with law enforcement and white supremacists), coupled with a particularly intense wildfire season. Beginning just before Labor Day in 2020, more than a million acres and 4,009 homes burned in Oregon. Portland was clouded in smoke for weeks while evacuation lines spread closer to metropolitan areas.

In the first stanza, "trumpet guy" refers to Camillo Massagli, an activist who became well-known in Portland and Seattle for bringing the trumpet his great-grandfather had given him to BLM demonstrations throughout 2020.

Page 37—"walking alone" takes its setting from the rainforest and sandspit beach found where the Salmon River meets the Pacific Ocean at Three Rocks just north of Lincoln City, Oregon. This Oregon coastal area is traditional and ancestral lands of the Siletz and Grande Ronde tribes.

Page 41—"planetesimals or skipping stones in atmosphere" is a cento drawn almost entirely from lines read by poets at online gatherings during the early pandemic. Throughout this time I made a listening practice of capturing a few gut-punch lines which I'd combine into brief collages of the collective energy we'd shared. As stanzas accumulated, I began to notice that, curated together, an evocative zeitgeist emerged. Footnotes credit line origins. Many lines were freshly penned in generative writing space. For lines from live readings of published work, please find sources on page 98. I offer this communal poem with big love to the writers quoted (and many others who were present and read poetry at these events) for the ways we gathered, shared, created and held it all together.

Page 55—"*but can novelty be our gender?*" takes its setting from Collins Beach on the northeast shore of Sauvie Island, the largest island along the Columbia River. Inhabitants once included more than 2,000 members of the Multnomah tribe of the Chinook Indians who call this place Wapato Island (or Wappatoo Island) in homage to the eponymous tuber which abundantly grew as a central food source. The Chinook know the Columbia River as Wimahl (or Wimal), "the big river."

Page 58—"this is what i will tell them" was written after astrologer Chani Nicholas's reading of Chiron's placement for my rising sign.

Page 63—"when we master that space between" was written in response to Andra Vltavín's "Chronic and Acute." The title line "when we master that space between" is Vltavín's.

Page 70—"nothing is stopping us" was written for my paternal grandfather William E. Goodwin (August 22, 1934–January 13, 2020). Mount St. Helens, a still active volcano known to the Klickitat people as Louwala-Clough ("smoking/fire mountain"), fills the eastward skyscape while looking out over the Columbia River into the state of Washington from my hometown, St. Helens, Oregon.

Page 75—"if you see us dancing know" was written after Lunita Valeria Velásquez's "self sourced life stoke." The line "and if you see me dancing just know" is Velásquez's.

Page 84—"greedy" includes reference to Wy'East—the Multnomah tribe's name for the volcanic peak visible from their ancestral homeland in the Columbia River (Wimahl or Wimal) basin—later coined Mount Hood by colonizer explorers in the 1790s (around the same time as its last eruptive activity).

Cascadia Department of Bio Region notes, "the native names for the mountains tell an engaging story, where the Cascade range becomes a community of dynamic and interconnected characters [...] explaining how the land was formed and the millennia long relationship people have had with it. Many of the peaks have multiple names, a reality reflected by the diversity of languages present across Cascadia, and relativity with which the mountains are viewed from across the region."

As Louse Erdrich expresses through her character Zhaanat in *The Night Watchman*, "Things started going wrong, as far as Zhaanat was concerned, when places everywhere were named for people—political figures, priests, explorers—and not for the real things that happened in these places—the dreaming, the eating, the death, the appearance of animals. This confusion of the chimookomaanag between the timelessness of the earth and the short span here of mortals was typical of their arrogance."

The lands now designated Mt. Hood National Forest are rightfully the territory of Indigenous nations including the Wishram, Wyam, Tenino, Walla-Walla, Wasco, Clackamas, Molalla, Taih, Chinook, Paiute, Kalapuya and others.

At the time of publication, the Confederated Tribes of Warm Springs face on ongoing water crisis. Donations can be made by searching "Chúush Fund." Additionally, living descendants of the Kalapuya are reviving their language from the brink of extinction (the last known fluent speaker of Kalapuya died in the 1950s). Donations can be made to this project by searching "Kalapuya dictionary."

Page 86—"awake" was written after a live reading by Julia Bray on the Taurus New Moon of June, 2020. The phrase "cosmic back-up" is Bray's.

SOURCES

"6 out-of-this-world celestial bodies you need to know." *CBC Kids* (2021). https://www.cbc.ca/kidscbc2/the-feed/six-out-of-this-world-celestial-bodies-you-need-to-know

"Asteroid Belt—Wikipedia." *En.Wikipedia.Org* (2021). https://en.wikipedia.org/wiki/Asteroid_belt.

Bass, Ellen. "The Thing Is." *Poetry of Presence: An Anthology of Mindfulness Poems* (Eds. Phyllis Cole-Dai & Ruby R Wilson, Grayson Books, 2017).

brown, adrienne maree. *Pleasure Activism: The Politics of Feeling Good* (AK Press, 2019).

Chien, Colette. "after Jenny Xie, zuihitsu—" *the melt* (2021). https://www.coletterae.com/the-melt

Chien, Colette. "On Top of the Earth Resting in Uncertainty." *The Rising Phoenix Review* (2020). https://therisingphoenixreview.com/2020/12/31/on-top-of-the-earth-resting-in-uncertainty-by-colette-chien/

Derricotte, Toi. "The Undertaking." *The Undertaker's Daughter* (Pitt Poetry Series: University of Pittsburgh Press, 2011).

Edera, Peg. "This World Is A Museum of Love." *Love Is Deeper than Distance: Poems of Love, Death, a Little Sex, ALS, Dementia and the Widow's Life Thereafter* (Fernwood Press, 2018).

Erdrich, Louise. *The Night Watchman* (HarperCollins, 2020).

Fiebig, Johannes. "5 of Cups." *Dalí. Tarot* (Taschen, 2003).

Florence + the Machine. "The End of Love." *High as Hope* (2018).

Franco, Bryan. "The Secret to Surviving Sinkholes." *Everything I Think Is All In My Mind* (Read Or Green Books, 2021).

Giménez Smith, Carmen. "Like an Autotune of Authentic Love." *Poem-a-Day* (Academy of American Poets, 2020). https://poets.org/poem/auto-tune-authentic-love

Goldberg, Lea. "And will they ever come…" *Selected Poetry and Drama* (Trans. Rachel Tzvia Back, Toby Press, 2005).

Gorman, Amanda. "In This Place: An American Lyric." *The Quarry: A Social Justice Poetry Database* (Split This Rock, 2017). https://www.splitthisrock.org/poetry-database/poem/in-this-place-an-american-lyric

Hancher, Gabby. "we are not prey." *High Priestesses of Poetry, Volume 2 Anthology* (2021).

Hancher, Gabby. "when you are a body." *The Growth Lines* (First Matter Press, 2021).

Hass, Ryan, Sergio Olmos and Jonathan Levinson. "Hate-group rally breaks up in Portland, turnout far below expectations." *Oregon Public Broadcasting*

(2020). https://www.opb.org/article/2020/09/26/live-updates-portland-under-state-of-emergency-as-hate-group-holds-rally/

Jackson, Major. "Let Me Begin Again." *Poem-a-Day* (Academy of American Poets, 2021). https://poets.org/poem/let-me-begin-again

Kostenko, Lena. "Chernobyl Poems." *Words Without Borders* (Trans. Uilleam Blacker, 2016). https://www.wordswithoutborders.org/dispatches/article/chernobyl-poems-lina-kostenko-uilleam-blacker

Le Guin, Ursula K. "Leaves." *So Far So Good: Poems 2014-2018* (Copper Canyon Press, 2018).

Mason, Holaday. "Virus. Virus. I love you." *High Priestesses of Poetry, Volume 3 Anthology* (2021).

Mojgani, Anis. "The Tree." *In the Pockets of Small Gods* (Write Bloody Publishing, 2018).

Native Land (Digital). https://native-land.ca/

"Native Place Names—How Wy'east (Mount Hood) Came To Be." Cascadia Department of Bio-Region (2019). https://cascadiabioregion.org/department-of-bioregion/jizehqoqc2pmu4va9lr8gdhnujdyeg

Notarianni, John, and Rolando Hernandez. "Bringing Oregon's Kalapuya language back from the brink of extinction." *Oregon Public Broadcasting* (2022). https://www.opb.org/article/2022/04/02/oregon-kalapuya-language-indigenous-people-willamette-valley-dictionary-native-americans/

Ríos, Alberto. "We Are of a Tribe." *Not Go Away Is My Name* (Copper Canyon Press, 2020).

Scarry, Elaine. *Dreaming By the Book* (Princeton University Press, 1999).

Schwarz, Andra. "I can't find them"; "I come from the forest"; "I forget my voice." *In the morning we are glass* (Trans. Caroline Wilcox Reul, Zephyr Press, 2021).

Straw, Timmy. "Copernicus." *Poem-a-Day* (Academy of American Poets, 2021). https://poets.org/poem/copernicus

Szymborska, Wisława. "Motion." *Poems, New and Collected, 1957-1997* (Ecco, 2000).

Velásquez, Lunita Valeria. "self sourced life stoke"; "the skeletons have been coming out." *High Priestesses of Poetry, Volume 2 Anthology* (2021).

Wakefield, Buddy. "We Were Emergencies." *Live at the Typer Canyon Grand* (2009).

Wani, Sanna. "Tomorrow Is a Place." *Poem-a-Day* (Academy of American Poets, 2021). https://poets.org/poem/tomorrow-place

Wiencek, Dan. "Archeology: A Beginner's Guide." *Routes Between Raindrops* (First Matter Press, 2021).

zaslavsky, ahuva s. "Summer Gestures"; "The Great Regression." *Between These Borders Wanders a Golem* (First Matter Press, 2022).

ACKNOWLEDGMENTS

Grateful acknowledgments to the following publications in which these poems first appeared, sometimes in earlier versions:

45th Parallel: "we meant for that to happen," "an entire world depends on you consistently dreaming yourself alive"

Birdcoat Quarterly: "sound of *stay* & *grow* come out of the same mouth," "want for beauty that could kill me"

Blood Tree Literature: "when we master that space between"

Cathexis Northwest Press: "us? beautiful / prepared for our own demise," "relieved to be small in a wave that will never relent," "nothing is stopping us"

Cimarron Review: "greedy"

deLuge Literary and Arts Journal: "let us wake different"

Faultline Journal of Arts & Letters: "i don't want to be careful," "what trance parts the sea at its own will?"

Gulf Stream Magazine: "theme park polaroids"

High Priestesses of Poetry, Volume 1 Anthology: "something heroic about curling into a fetal position to hold the multiverse under the bed"

High Priestesses of Poetry, Volume 2 Anthology: "altar offering to what we cannot know," "so many things we must be alone enough for," "if you see us dancing know," "it takes light years to get around things"

High Priestesses of Poetry, Volume 3 Anthology: "taut center / loose edges," "look at you baby self," "awake"

House Journal: "this is what it feels like to love"

Imposter: A Poetry Journal: "this is what i will tell them"

Not Very Quiet: "'i haven't"

Potted Purple: "'are you in touch with," "happening everywhere all at the same time," "the realness of body," "when we master that space between" (reprint)

Rise Up Review: "but can novelty be our gender?"

Timberline Review: "my third grade teacher isn't squeamish"

The Cape Rock: "we move & stars blur," "what i apprehend of time travel" (reprint)

Voicemail Poems: "what i apprehend of time travel"

Wild Roof Journal: "serious child"

Willawaw Journal: "walking alone"

These poems arise out of my relationship to and lived experiences on Earth, with blessings to its oceans, rivers, trees, creatures, spirits and all people who have tended this place and space since time immemorial. My homeland is stolen traditional and ancestral lands of the Multnomah, Clackamas, Chinook, Kathlamet, Tualatin Kalapuya, Molalla and many other tribes and bands of the Columbia and Willamette regions. May we recognize a collective responsibility to listen to and work in solidarity with sovereign Indigenous communities to heal the traumas and thefts of colonialism. Words are not enough. Action and investment are required—*LANDBACK*.

I am grateful and privileged to learn about liberation and anti-racism from the labor and scholarship of countless Black thought-leaders, writers and teachers including: adrienne maree brown, Octavia E. Butler, Resmaa Menakem, Reverend angel Kyodo Williams, bell hooks and others. Words are not enough. Action and investment are required—*REPARATIONS*.

These poems exist because of generative writing space cocreators and are more focused and fully alive from the investment of craft workshop collaborators: Andra Vltavín, Neil Aitken, Beth Melnick, Emily Dempsey, ahuva s. zaslavsky, Holaday Mason, Skyler Reed, Rhonda Nichols, Lunita Valeria Velásquez, Samantha Cimino, Gabby Hancher, Jenn Lalime, Dawn Thompson, Sierra Vida Lisa, Birch Dwyer, Lauren Paredes, Caroline Wilcox Reul, Emily Moon, Dan Wiencek, Andrew Chenevert and many others.

To Gail Wronsky, Chuck Rosenthal, Karen Kevorkian and all the fine folks at What Books Press—thank you for all I've learned as we've brought so many books to life together since 2009. And thank you for believing in this one.

To Gronk—for the generosity of your art.

To Dawn, Abs, Els & Pi—being your aunt is the best.

To my ancestors, family, pops, Jeffy & especially my mama—
love you all around the universe.

To J., S. & T.—you're my people forevs.

 ASH GOOD is a nonbinary queer poet & designer living, playing & working in Portland, OR. They are the author of five books/chapbooks, cofounding editor at First Matter Press (a 501c3 nonprofit) & a reader for *Frontier Poetry*. Their poetry has been nominated for Best of the Net & appears in *Faultline Journal of Arts & Letters, Cimarron Review, 45th Parallel, Chautauqua, Bird Coat Quarterly, Gulf Stream Magazine, Voicemail Poems* & others. ASHGOOD.COM

WHAT BOOKS PRESS

LOS ANGELES

2022

No One Dies in Palmyra Ohio
HENRY ELIZABETH CHRISTOPHER
NOVEL

Us Clumsy Gods
ASH GOOD
POEMS

Skeletal Lights From Afar
FORREST ROTH
FLASH FICTION/PROSE POEMS

That Blue Trickster Time
AMY UYEMATSU
POEMS

2021

Pyre
MAUREEN ALSOP
POEMS

What Falls Away is Always
HAAKE & WRONSKY, EDITORS
ESSAYS

The Eight Mile Suspended Carnival
REBECCA KUDER
NOVEL

Game
M.L. WILLIAMS
POEMS

2020

No, Don't
ELENA KARINA BYRNE
POEMS

One Strange Country
STELLA HAYES
POEMS

*Remembering Dismembrance:
A Critical Compendium*
DANIEL TAKESHI KRAUSE
NOVEL

Keeping Tahoe Blue
ANDREW TONKAVICH
STORIES

2019

Time Crunch
CATHY COLMAN
POEMS

Whole Night Through
L.I. HENLEY
POEMS

Echo Under Story
KATHERINE SILVER
NOVEL

Decoding Sparrows
MARIANO ZARO
POEMS

2018

Interrupted by the Sea
PAUL LIEBER
POEMS

The Headwaters of Nirvana
BILL MOHR
POEMS

2017

*Gary Oldman Is a Building
You Must Walk Through*
FORREST ROTH
NOVEL

Rhombus and Oval
JESSICA SEQUEIRA
STORIES

Imperfect Pastorals
GAIL WRONSKY
POEMS

2016

The Mysterious Islands
A.W. DEANNUNTIS
STORIES

The "She" Series: A Venice Correspondence
HOLADAY MASON & SARAH MACLAY
POEMS

Mirage Industries
CAROLIE PARKER
POEMS

2015

*The Balloon Containing the Water
Containing the Narrative Begins Leaking*
RICH IVES
STORIES

The Shortest Farewells Are the Best
CHUCK ROSENTHAL & GAIL WRONSKY
LITERARY COLLAGE/PROSE POEMS

2014

It Looks Worse Than I Am
LAURIE BLAUNER
POEMS

They Become Her
REBBECCA BROWN
NOVEL

*The Final Death of Rock-and-Roll
& Other Stories*
A.W. DEANNUNTIS
STORIES

Perfecta
PATTY SEYBURN
POEMS

2013

Brittle Star
ROD VAL MOORE
NOVEL

Sex Libris
JUDITH TAYLOR
POEMS

Start With A Small Guitar
LYNNE THOMPSON
POEMS

Tomorrow You'll Be One of Us
WRONSKY, ROSENTHAL, GRONK
ART/LITERARY COLLAGE/POEMS

2012

The Mermaid at the Americana Arms Motel
A.W. DEANNUNTIS
NOVEL

The Time of Quarantine
KATHARINE HAAKE
NOVEL

Frottage & Even As We Speak
MONA HOUGHTON
NOVELLAS

*West of Eden:
A Life in 21st Century Los Angeles*
CHUCK ROSENTHAL
MAGIC JOURNALISM

2010

Master Siger's Dream
A.W. DEANNUNTIS
NOVEL

Other Countries
RAMÓN GARCÍA
POEMS

A Giant Claw
GRONK
ART
ESSAY BY GAIL WRONSKY
SPANISH TRANSLATION
BY ALICIA PARTNOY

Coyote O'Donohughe's History of Texas
CHUCK ROSENTHAL
NOVEL

So Quick Bright Things
GAIL WRONSKY
POEMS
BILINGUAL, SPANISH TRANSLATION
BY ALICIA PARTNOY

2009

Bling & Fringe (The L.A. Poems)
MOLLY BENDALL & GAIL WRONSKY
POEMS

April, May, and So On
FRANÇOIS CAMOIN
STORIES

One of Those Russian Novels
KEVIN CANTWELL
POEMS

*The Origin of Stars
& Other Stories*
KATHARINE HAAKE
STORIES

Lizard Dream
KAREN KEVORKIAN
POEMS

*Are We Not There Yet? Travels in
Nepal, North India, and Bhutan*
CHUCK ROSENTHAL
MAGIC JOURNALISM

As a small, independent press, we urge our readers to support independent booksellers. This is easily done on our website by purchasing our books either through Indiebound or from BookShop.

WHATBOOKSPRESS.COM

www.ingramcontent.com/pod-product-compliance
Lightning Source LLC
Chambersburg PA
CBHW020542080526
44583CB00013B/946